H is for HBCU's

Henry Benton, III

Illustrated by Jasmine Moseley

www.TrueVinePublishing.org

H is for HBCUs
By Henry Benton, III
Illustration by: Jasmine Moseley

Published by True Vine Publishing Co.
P.O. Box 22448, Nashville, TN 37202
www.TrueVinePublishing.org

ISBN: 978-1-7375934-1-5

Copyright@2021 by Hank Benton, III
All rights reserved. No part of this book may be reproduced, scanned, or distributed in any printed or electronic form without permission. Please do not participate in or encourage piracy or copyrighted materials in violation of the author's rights.

Dedication

This book is dedicated to all Historically Black Colleges and Universities, the Black alumni who attended any of them, and future attendees of them. Your dreams are in reach. Dream often. Dream big. Dream Black!

Special shout out to Tennessee State University. Go Big Blue!

A is for Alabama State University.

D is for **Dr. Martin Luther King Jr.**, Civil Rights pioneer who graduated from **Morehouse College**.

G is for Grambling State University.

I is for **Inventor, Lonnie Johnson,** graduate of **Tuskegee University,** inventor of the Super Soaker.

J is for **Julian Manly Earls,** the first African American section head, office chief and deputy director of the NASA Glenn Research Center, graduate of **Norfolk State University.**

L is for **Langston Hughes**, historical poet and novelist who graduated from **Lincoln University**.

M is for Meharry Medical College.

N is for North Carolina A&T State University.

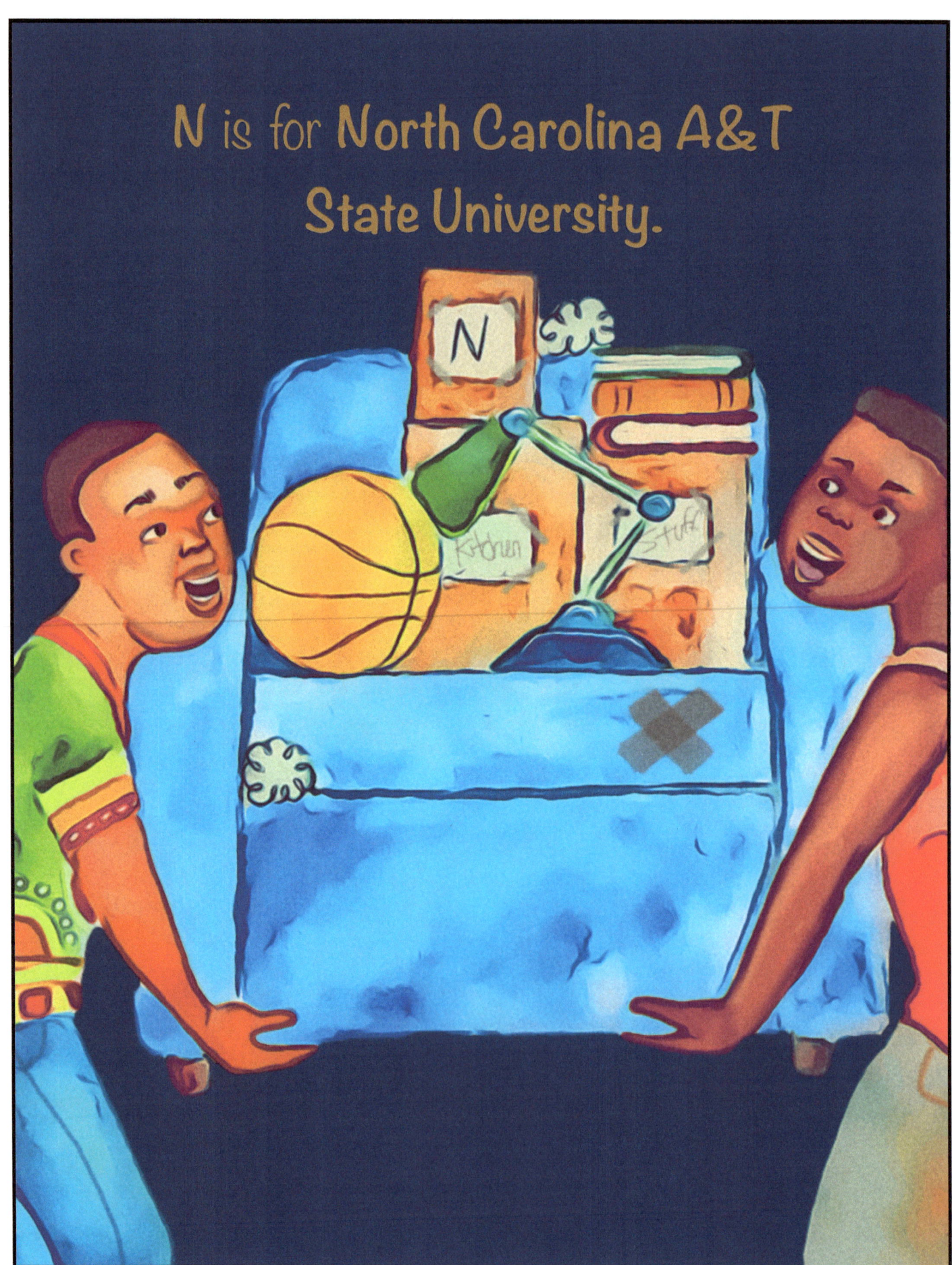

O is for **Oprah Winfrey**, who attended **Tennessee State University**.

Q is for Queen, television miniseries written by Alex Haley, who attended Alcorn State University & Elizabeth City State College.

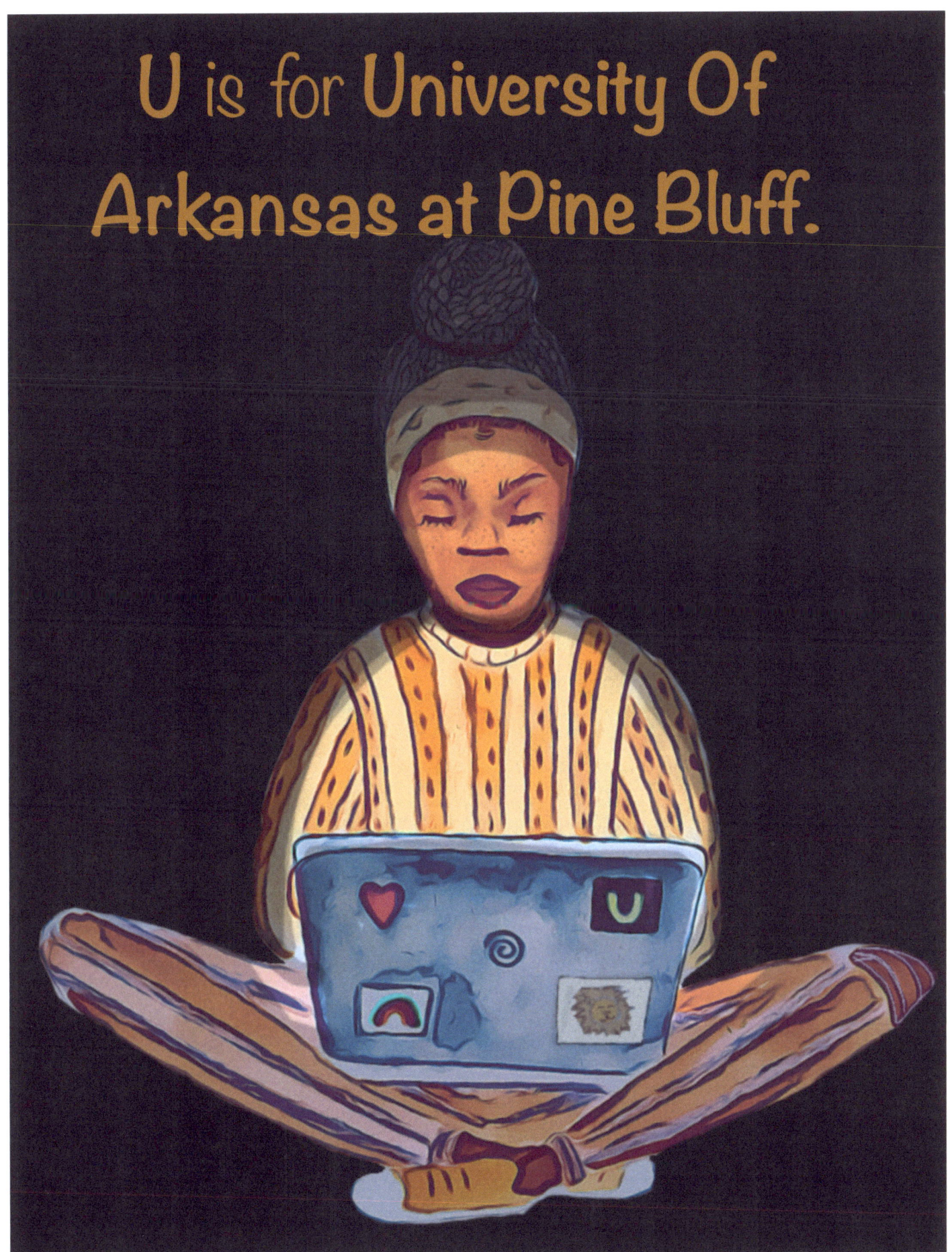

U is for University Of Arkansas at Pine Bluff.

V is for **Vice President Kamala Harris**, first African American & woman Vice President of the United States of America who graduated from **Howard University.**

W is for Walter Payton, NFL Hall of Fame running back who graduated from **Jackson State University**.

X is for Xavier University of Louisiana.

Y is for **Yolanda Adams**, award winning gospel singer who graduated from **Texas Southern University**.

Z is for **Zora Neale Hurston**, author and filmmaker, graduate of **Howard University**.

HBCU's of America

Alabama
Alabama A & M University
Alabama State University
Bishop State Community Coll.
Concordia College- Selma
Gadsden State Comm. College
Trenholm State Technical Coll.
J. F. Drake State Technical Coll.
Lawson State Comm. College
Miles College
Oakwood University
Selma University
Shelton State Comm. College
Stillman College
Talladega College
Tuskegee University

Arkansas
Arkansas Baptist College
Philander Smith College
Univ. of Arkansas at Pine Bluff
Shorter College

California
Charles R. Drew University of Medicine and Science

Delaware
Delaware State University

Florida
Bethune-Cookman University
Edward Waters College
Florida A&M University
Florida Memorial University

Georgia
Albany State University
Clark Atlanta University
Fort Valley State University
Interdenominational Theological Ctr.
Morehouse College
Morehouse School of Medicine
Morris Brown College
Paine College
Savannah State University
Spelman College

Kentucky
Kentucky State University
Simmons College

Louisiana
Dillard University
Grambling State University
Southern Univ. and A&M College
Southern Univ. at New Orleans
Southern Univ. at Shreveport
Xavier University of Louisiana

Maryland
Bowie State University
Coppin State University
Morgan State University
Univ. of Maryland, Eastern Shore

Missouri
Harris-Stowe State University
Lincoln University

Mississippi
Alcorn State University
Coahoma Community College
Hinds Community College-Utica
Jackson State University
Mississippi Valley State University
Rust College
Tougaloo College

North Carolina
Barber-Scotia College
Bennett College
Elizabeth City State Univ.
Fayetteville State University
Johnson C. Smith University
Livingstone College
North Carolina A&T Univ.
North Carolina Central Univ.

St. Augustine's College
Shaw University
Winston Salem State University

Ohio
Central State University
Wilberforce University

Oklahoma
Langston University

Pennsylvania
Cheyney University
Lincoln University

South Carolina
Allen University
Benedict College
Claflin University
Clinton College
Denmark Technical College
Morris College
South Carolina State University
Voorhees College

Tennessee
American Baptist College
Fisk University
Knoxville College
Lane College
LeMoyne-Owen College
Meharry Medical College
Tennessee State University

Texas
Huston-Tillotson Univ.
Jarvis Christian College
Paul Quinn College
Prairie View A&M Univ.
Southwestern Christian Coll.
Texas College
Texas Southern University
Wiley College

Virgin Islands
Univ. of the Virgin Island

Virginia
Hampton University
Norfolk State University
Saint Paul's College
Virginia State University
Virginia Union University
Virginia Univ. of Lynchburg

Washington, DC
Howard University
Howard College of Medicine
Univ. of the District of Columbia

West Virginia
Bluefield State College
West Virginia State Univ.